How to Improve Your Personality

Techniques and Self Help Tips to Improve Personality and Confidence

By Camon Dlyde

How to Improve Your Personality
Techniques and Self Help Tips to Improve Personality and Confidence
by **Camon Dlyde**

Printed in the United States of America

Copyright © 2010 **Camon Dlyde**

All rights reserved. Except for use in a review, no portion of this book may be reproduced in any form without the express written permission of the author.

Neither the author nor the publisher assumes any responsibility for the use or misuse of information contained in this book.

LEGAL NOTICE:

The Publisher has attempted to be as accurate and complete as possible in the creation of this book, notwithstanding the fact that he does not warrant or represent at any time that the contents within are accurate due to the rapidly changing nature of the topic.

While all attempts have been made to verify information provided in this publication, the Publisher assumes no responsibility for errors, omissions, or contrary interpretation of the subject matter herein. Any perceived slights of specific persons, peoples, or organizations are unintentional.

In practical advice books, like anything else in life, there are no guarantees of results. Readers are cautioned to rely on their own judgment about their individual circumstances to act accordingly.

This book is not intended for use as a source of legal, business, accounting or financial advice. All readers are advised to seek services of competent professionals in legal, business, accounting, medical, and finance field.

Table of Contents

How to Get to Know Yourself Better Than Now	1
How to Discover Your Personality?	3
Know Yourself	5
Each Person is Distinct and Special	5
Supervising Your Virtues and Vices i.e. Your Features	6
How Law of Attraction Helps in Personal Development	7
Do You Have A Positive Attitude? Take the Quiz	9
The Success of your Business Depends on your Positive Attitude	12
Develop the Ideal Personality for Success in Business	16
Maintaining Positive Attitude	19
Maintain a Positive Attitude During Hard Times	22
What You Need to Be on the Top	25
Traits of a Dynamic Personality	27
Learn to Face Criticisms	31
Those Who Truly Believes in You and Want to Help You Out	31
Those Who Do Not Have Your Best Interest at Heart	32
Personality Style Differences Between Managers and Leaders	34

Do You Have The Personality To Innovate?	38
Keep a Check on Your Attitude	41
Anger	41
EOE – Instant Expert On Everything	42
Refusal of Taking Responsibility for Your Own Actions	43
AAMS- the All about Me Syndrome	43
Minimizing the Seriousness of Your Effect on Others	44
How to Get Rid of Shyness	44
Venture out	45
Get the Right Body Language	46
Give Those Personality Development Classes a Try	46
Keep on Trying	47

How to Improve Your Personality

How to Get to Know Yourself Better Than Now

We meet new people everyday, for work or otherwise—whether we interact with them or not, you develops instinctive likes and dislikes towards people. This has lot to do with their personality.

To think that your personality is made up of only the way you look would be anomalous however. Your ideas, the way you think, your priorities in life, your emotions all comprise your personality. You need to understand and accept yourself the way you are if you want to be happy.

You can take a personality test to help you figure out what kind of personality you have. A substantial number of these are available online and in different books. Think about how much you know yourself. What are the things that are important for you?

Put all societal and familial expectations aside for a minute and think about what you really want to do, what would make you happy? Knowing yourself well is important and will serve you well in various situations.

How to Improve Your Personality

When you are looking for a job, for example, it would be ideal to not get stuck with something that you don't want to do. Knowing yourself would also help you accept other people as they are. It will help you develop an open mind.

One way or the other, the ultimate thing is to do things that are important for you and that make you happy. If you are an introvert, you should regularly spend quality time by yourself. You can also keep your diary, if you are uncomfortable sharing your deeper thoughts with other people. Don't hesitate to stand by what you believe in.

This is important for you to be happy. It will be good for you to develop a constructive hobby. If you are introvert don't succumb to peer pressure and compulsively spend time with people. Learn how to say no. Draw lines around you and your space as and when you need to.

Extroverts on the other hand should get involved in group activities like theatre for example. Learn new things whenever possible. Don't hesitate to experiment. Stay in regular touch with your friends and family.

If you have any introvert friends learn to accept them as they are.

In your growing up years, a lot of things that are going on around you, go into shaping your personality. Some experts also believe that a lot of genetic factors go into making you who you are. But the important thing is to accept yourself the way you are.

If there are certain things about you that you don't like however, you can try to make minor alterations.

How to Discover Your Personality?

One of the most significant aspects of the modern world is the way you look and carry yourself. People are much inclined to appear like the movie stars or models of any fashionable person that they admire.

How to Improve Your Personality

These famous personalities are considered to be paragons of fashion and beauty. But we always need to keep in mind that beauty is not just about wearing the right dress and looking hip.

The most important factor that fashions beauty is your personality. We hardly look into this factor anymore. Once your personality is refined, you will have mastered eternal beauty.

Research reveals that men, often, prefer people who might not be very good looking but are sweet, interactive and trustworthy. Thus this shows that women who are not considered to be conventionally beautiful but have great personalities do attract a lot of attention.

It is not a conflict between personality and good looks. Allow both these aspects in to mature simultaneously and you will notice that your personally will accentuate your good looks and vice versa.

Know Yourself

The primary thing that you need to do is understand yourself. It is essential for you to comprehend your personality in order to refine it and thus improve your physical beauty. Let the process be slow and gradual.

You can also consult the various books and other content that is available – they will help you locate your character. Opt for the examinations as well as the help teams that are found on the test to know yourself better.

Each Person is Distinct and Special

One person can always consider another person's character and attitude in a negative light. Often people consider hyperactive or unusually quiet people to be crazy or odd. This notion is rather relative- each one appears little strange to another person. You can always utilize your attitude to improve yourself.

Supervising Your Virtues and Vices i.e. Your Features

Sort out your virtues and vices. Be a good person and get rid of all your negative points..
Focus on your virtues. If you wish to make your personality an instrument in order to be more appealing, then surely concentrate on your virtues and let your virtues be the attention centre. Each person is special and distinct in his or her own way. So let the good in you shine in front of others!

Personality is an essential component of the self of a person. By perfecting your personality you will be able to reveal the beauty that lies within you.

Personality is not distinct from your external beauty. It is just an external manifestation of your internal splendor. It is important for you to let people understand that beauty is not just about good looks. An impressive personality is equally significant!

How Law of Attraction Helps in Personal Development

Laws of attraction can be very crucial when you are trying to understand your personality and its development. Failures and successes are a part of life and should be taken in the same spirit.

The ideal thing is to take all your failures as lessons for your life. Take these incidents to understand your limitations and things that you did wrong and try not to repeat them in the future. This is how you can pave the way for your success.

Deal with your failures as and when they occur. To keep them locked inside you and drag them along wherever you go will only complicate your present and future.

What you think is what you are, is one of the most important laws of attraction. If you are always surrounded by negative, pessimistic thoughts it will hamper your growth and personality development.

How to Improve Your Personality

Given below are some things you need to consider and sought out if you are working towards a positive personality:

Learn you accept yourself the way you are. You might have shortcomings and limitations but so does everybody else. If you can't love yourself, how will you love and accept other people.
No matter how many things are going wrong around you, learn to take control. The moment start pitying yourself, you have lost half the battle already.

Even if you are surrounded by people who have a lot of negativity don't let it get to you. Try and make them see the brighter side of life if possible. But learn to step away as and when they start getting to you.

No matter how messed up things are, tomorrow would be a new day and a new beginning. Stop mulling over your failures and try to fix things the best you can.

It's important to set goals for yourself. But make sure that the goals are realistic. Also reward yourself as and when you achieve desired results.

Learn to be confident about yourself. If you are sure about what you want go ahead and get it. Don't let anything put you down.

Developing your personality means discovering your weaknesses and working on them. Learning from your failures and making sure that you don't commit the same mistakes again and again in crucial.

Learn to be good to yourself and do things that make you happy. If you are good to people then you would *attract the same kind of behavior and people*. Learn to be positive and happy and everything will start to look up.

Do You Have A Positive Attitude? Take the Quiz

This chapter presents the latest information on positive attitude. It is designed to either reconfirm your knowledge or enhance your knowledge on the subject by routing your thoughts on positive attitude through 5 questions.

1. Am I happy being where I am today?

This is a trick question without any standard answer, but knowing how to deal with it is crucial: for believing that you are happy can actually increase your happiness and contentment, and give you the confidence and positive attitude for anything that you wish to achieve. So do not simply wish to be happy but come out and believe that you really are: enjoy and be thankful for the little things in life and see what a difference it makes.

2. Am I appealing to the opposite sex?

Even if you do not have an answer to this, it shouldn't stop you from doing anything you wish. So be it shaping up, changing your dressing style or hairdo, your attitude towards people or life, do it as if you were appealing, and it shall conduce to your benefit. Remember that what matters the most is how well you can carry it off rather than exactly what you are trying to carry off.

3. How much could I have?

Operative here is not a standard that could define having too much or having too little, but rather how the question of how badly you really need or desire it. This boils down to asking yourself what, and how much, you are willing to work and sacrifice for something you think you want. If you really are willing to sweat for it, then no matter what, work on towards what you have set your heart on and the sky is the limit.

4. What motivates me?

Human desires are endless, and there are infinite variations to the things that make people happy. If you do not know what drives you or sets your pulse racing, approach life like a buffet service. Try everything piece by piece until you locate your favorite dish.

5. What Really Makes You Tick?

Understanding what really makes you tick is to not only be able to define your goal but also the path that you seek to chart towards that goal. So identify what you really want and what you are willing to do for it. It's all about knowing yourself; you own limits and doing your own cost benefit analysis, rather than any very profoundly philosophic quest.

The Success of your Business Depends on your Positive Attitude

Your business will prosper greatly if you build and consequently sustain a positive attitude. Even when things in your business are not going according to plan, you have to remember that you are not alone. All business ventures have their ups and downs.

Those impediments can be easily overcome and you can always get back on track if you keep a positive outlook to everything. You will also have increased confidence in yourself and your business capabilities.

A positive attitude will make finding prospective customers simpler. Others will react well to your optimism. They will want to hire you and suggest you to others.

This will also assist you in other departments of life. You will be in good health. Positive people have less fear of heart inflictions.

Here are some useful tips for you to expand on your positive attitude.

- **Be Nice to Others:** Being polite and friendly with other individuals will make you feel nice about yourself. You will have a brilliant and happy day. However, you shouldn't be gullible and allow people to manipulate you because of your friendliness.

- **Mix with Other Positive People and Avoid Those who Have Negative Attitudes:** Attitudes rub on to others very quickly. If you spend more of your time with positive people you will automatically find yourself developing a more optimistic attitude.

However, negative attitudes can also be very infectious. There is a popular saying which goes, "Misery loves company". When you are always in the company of people who perpetually complain, you will automatically find yourself beginning to do the same. Insignificant factors that would normally not bother you will suddenly seem to spoil your entire day. You will feel like you have lost all your energy.

The moment you lose enthusiasm and incentive, it can prove very difficult to get back on track. These factors can take a negative toll on your business. You will not get anything constructive done this way.

- **Be Organized and Practice Time Management:** When you are systematic you will work faster and be able to complete more tasks. You will know exactly what you need to do achieve your target each day. You will do constructive work if you stay within a system instead wasting time searching for phone numbers or email addresses that you have misplaced.

- **Be Proactive:** The moment you are aware of an oncoming obstacle in your work, solve it instead of leaving it till the last instant. Be practical and have a solution ready before the problem can get out of hand. By being ahead of possible impediments, you will permanently be able to avoid setbacks.

- **Consider Hiring a Coach:** Many individuals hire tutors nowadays to attain success in business. These tutors of guides will assist you in deciding exactly what you require your business to yield. They will set attainable targets and will also demand justifications for actions.

Therefore, the right and positive attitude is the most important ingredient for a successful business. Practice it as well as follow it daily. You'll soon see you have become much more successful than you ever conceived of.

Develop the Ideal Personality for Success in Business

A few days back when my associate informed me about this fresh advertising organization and also acquainted me with their webpage, I immediately looked into it. Well, it was absolutely detestable!

It definitely had pretty pictures and a flashy look but the write up could hardly be read or understood. The webpage was designed craftily but was not a user friendly webpage.

The webpage was pathetic as it lacked a unique personality. It had no distinctive feature or that zing to hold my attention. The write up was quite uninteresting and so were the apparently lovely pictures. The write-up consisted of too many We's! The website lacked vitality and enthusiasm. It was a bit too perfect in its endeavor to impress all and thus could impress none!

People generally wish to conduct trade with people they have faith in and are fond of. You need to understand that people will be fond of you only when your personality impresses them. There is no use at all concealing your true personality behind the veil of that silly, dull and dreary website! People will never get to be acquainted with you this way and they will also not wait for you for too long.

According to Dan Kennedy, if you are dull and tedious in your advertising plans then it will lead you absolutely nowhere. No one will bother to pay you any attention if you are uninteresting. Most people will not even turn to look twice- there is so much more to do in life and so many other interesting things to look into!

Well these questions are now forming clouds in your mind: how will I work things out in case am not appreciated or in case I put off potential buyers? Well this might be the case with you and it probably should too. I shall explain why I incorporate the word "SHOULD".

The moment you are writing a note that is so sugar coated, you should immediately realize that it will be extremely dull and will attract none. In your endeavor to make it appealing, you will actually put off people. Your note will not incite

How to Improve Your Personality

any enthusiasm and hence you will not receive any clients. They would prefer someone who is adequately interesting.

Peter Montoya says that a nice label can excite people and also similarly fend them off. Hence if your organization is not resisting a certain crowd, then it is also not attracting your potential customers in a way it should.

Deter those people who would not be attracted to your personality or your commodities generally and yet wish to conduct business with you. Fend them off right from the start because they will never be fond of someone of your personality or be satisfied with your merchandise. It will never be a good deal!

Business is not just about formalities and official statements. This is the conventional view about business. You might be little apprehensive in the beginning but know that the more thrilling and stimulating your web content as well as write up is, the more popular will be the response to it.

So you understand that your personality needs to blend in your label. Here you ask yourself "how do I go about this?". Well you will have to wait awhile- look into your inbox! I shall be giving you certain hints and suggestions in the upcoming copy.

Maintaining Positive Attitude

Successful people are identifiable by their masterful positive attitude, which makes it appear as if there's nothing that they couldn't achieve if they wanted and nothing they couldn't possess! It is a positive attitude which separates the successful from the losers: a self realized energy that propels towards success as opposed to a self defeating one that creates problems and provokes suffering in life.

Positive attitude is a state and condition of your mind that allows you to handle stress with optimism and patience, promoting hope and nullifying despair. This empowers you to be undeterred by problems, maintain your focus and continue to persevere without frustration, and thus eventually overcome all problems.

So if you have been a pessimist and have been filled with negative thoughts, here's how to get rid of your problem, embrace your cherished goals and develop a positive attitude.

1. **When you sense any signs of negativity or pessimism creeping into your mind, immediately check your thoughts and stop:** Instead try to imagine and visualize your favorite memories, expectations or ideals.

2. **Experts recommend another way to banish negative thoughts from your mind, a mechanism which involves two basic stages:** The first which drives away negative thoughts and emotions, and the second which allows negativity to be infiltrated and overcome with positive thoughts and feelings.

3. **Talking to yourself and repeating positive affirmations are proven techniques to develop a positive mindset**. So devise your personal prep talk

and motivation statement and make it a point to talk to yourself regularly.

4. Another helpful way is to **make posters or sticky notes carrying positive and affirmative statements such as: I can do it, Success is mine, My goal is within reach, etc**, and to put them up around your home or workplace where you are apt see the message regularly, day and night.

5. **Try to make the highly successful people be your friends and acquaintances, and try and spend time with them and know their approach.** In the right company, its easy for the secret to a positive attitude to rub off onto you.

6. **Begin to read positive self help books and magazine, or better still the biographies or autobiographies of your heroes.** You could also attend relevant seminars and workshops.

Remember that a positive attitude can only be cultivated and maintained by you; it is wholly internal to you which no body can take away. It requires much time, effort and dedication, but is an invaluable asset.

Maintain a Positive Attitude During Hard Times

Often there are times when everything seems to go wrong despite one's hardest efforts. During these times, a positive attitude will assist a person to regain his stamina and come out of the rough patch easily.

You should never blame yourself for things that naturally seem to go wrong in life. These incidents cannot be avoided. You should always remember that tomorrow brings the hope of a new day.

Most days turn out to be positive for people, but there will always be occasional pitfalls when nothing seems to go right. Just take the failed day in your stride and move on ahead with the assurance that a better day will soon come.

Always let go of the distress of today and keep faith in the anticipation that tomorrow brings. Most of the days in an individual's life bring about

How to Improve Your Personality

positive results. If you can maintain a positive attitude regardless of what might happen, the bad days will be kept to a bare minimum.

Always remember that a positive attitude will help you recover quicker in times of distress. Some bad days will motivate you to have an even more positive attitude so that you can learn from the mistakes of today for a better tomorrow.

The situation may be extremely difficult. But a positive attitude will help you overcome irrespective of how bad the situation is and you will definitely regain your confidence and self respect.

Hard times will always appear in life. But they seem less hard when life is viewed optimistically. No matter how a hard life may seem at some stage, a positive attitude will help you keep your head clear and allow you to think steadily so that you can find the right solution.

Even at work, a positive attitude will help you keep your calm and you will be able to do all the tasks that need to be done to improve the situation. You will be able to end your day on an optimistic note.

Even when you are sick or in despair, a positive attitude will help you recover quicker. The illness or the disappointment will pass sooner. You should not break down simply because you don't feel fit and fine. Real strength and stamina come from learning to be optimistic and believing that time will soon change for the better.

No one is flawless. Making mistakes is a natural part of life. You have to learn from your wrongdoings and be prepared for the future. You should not always blame yourself and lose your composure when something goes wrong.

Make this a positive learning opportunity for the future. It is easy to maintain a positive attitude during smooth times. It is only when you can do the same during rougher times that you can achieve happiness and success much faster.

What You Need to Be on the Top

Have you noticed a certain kind of radiance and aura surrounding people who are successful and doing well in their lives?

Some people have one particular skill that they tap on for their success while some people have a whole range of plus points that work in their favor in their professional life and otherwise. Its important to identify things that you are good at and concentrate on them and to know how to work them in your favor.

Especially with regards to your professional life, it's important that you should be doing something that you truly love. If you are not sure about what it is that you really want don't be afraid to experiment. Look around. Spend time doing things that you haven't done before. This will also enable you to discover your strengths, weaknesses and interests.

Before everything else, you need to identify what success means to you. Largely speaking there are two spheres in which people seek to be successful

How to Improve Your Personality

—personal (relating to friends and family) and professional (relating to your field of work). Some skills are however useful for both these spheres.

It's important how you react to and act upon emotions. Its important to maintain your cool in all kinds of stress-ridden situations. People who maintain their calm are most likely to make logical decisions be in control.

Failures are a part of life. Learn to take them in your stride. It is ideal to learn from your mistakes. The key to success is that you should stop being afraid of failures. If you have a goal in your mind you have to persistent. Don't give up.

You have to be innovative and think out of the box. When faced with a problem retain your cool and think of all possible ways to tackle it.

Don't be afraid of fear. You might be afraid of doing new things and taking new challenges or of pushing yourself to new limits. This would also limit your success. Use your fear constructively.
The curiosity might have killed the cat but it is good for you.

Ask questions, when you are not sure about what is happening. It's important for you to get a clear picture of the happenings before you can even identify the problem and then eventually tackle it.

If you want to be successful, you need to inculcate level headedness patience. You need to be willing to learn from people around you and keep an open mind. Don't be afraid to do new things and think beyond conventional framework.

Traits of a Dynamic Personality

The right attitude not only defines who you are but also your stance and success in life. That is why all top of the line business owners are those who have in their lives been not just about physical, mental and social prowess, but about the right attitude, with regards to the nature of success and achievement and the need to achieve something in life.

Some of the primary qualities of a successful man are listed below for your perusal.

How to Improve Your Personality

1. **Powerful need to achieve** — This quality is not the entrepreneur's quantitative success score card about how much has been done. Neither is this just about gaining popularity through success. It is the basic need to do something in life to make it worthwhile to oneself and gain self respect in the eyes of others.

2. **Perseverance** — Getting an inspiration, no matter how vague, and standing by it to see the resultant end through, is a primary characteristic of a success story. This never-admit-defeat and always-be-determined aspect is the most defined stamp of a dynamic personality.

3. **Positive mental attitude** —There is nothing that speaks of success in a person more than his optimistic mindset. Every successful person has to endure hard times and challenges and this is the time when his optimism carries him forth.

4. **Objectivity** — Knowing ones self, knowing ones shortcomings and carrying on

accordingly, without getting emotionally affected is also a must have quality in a successful person. This will not only enable him to assess the pros and cons of a certain move mater of fact, but will also enable him to, without personal involvement, stand by or discard a project according to its qualities.

5. **Foresight** — Any successful person must have a gift of vision. This vision is not the divine or spiritual vision but the gift of anticipation and foresight. This quality if possessed allows a person to always b on guard and aware of all possible occurrences where business is concerned.

6. **Well-developed personal relations skills** — You are nothing without your clients and partners in any business venture. That is why being a people person, without overt involvement, is absolutely crucial for any successful business man.

7. **Strong communication skills** — You have ideas and you need to convey it to

others to make it a reality. But conveying does not mean that it will be accepted, so convincing has to be added to it. This is why the ability to communicate confidently, both on pen and paper and by word of mouth, is extremely important.

8. **Resourcefulness** — Instinctive ability to foresee problems and solve them, even though it is a never-heard-of-before-kind, is also a quality of the successful man. It hints at the ability of being aware and draw inspiration from immediate surroundings to deal with the matter at hand.

9. **Technical knowledge** — The know-how of your field, be it the technical aspect or the economic is extremely important for a businessman, this will enable him to be ahead of all situations and deal with possible problems in a well rounded manner.

10. **A respectful attitude towards money** — The ability to not equate money with success but with the means to do

something worthwhile is very important. This ensures that the successful man remains more than a mercenary at the end of the day and still appreciates the value of hard work and diligence.

So here in a nutshell are the qualities that make a man a living success story…do you have it in you to be one?

Learn to Face Criticisms

Everyone has faced some kind of criticism at some point in their lives for sure. No one in their sane head would call criticisms as fun. Rather they can turnout to be quite discouraging. You must keep a very positive attitude when it comes to criticisms. For doing this you must be aware of the two vital areas from where every form of criticism usually generates.

Those Who Truly Believes in You and Want to Help You Out

This is the type of criticism that usually hurts the most. No body likes the fact that you are being criticized by the people whom you love and respect the most.

However one must keep their intentions in mind. If someone is really close to you and want the best to happen to you, they would not sweet talk you for your mistakes.

When your closest ones criticize it is usually a constructive criticism and you must pay heed to that and if you feel that it is for your best interest then follow their suggestions and imply the adjustments they might offer.

Those Who Do Not Have Your Best Interest at Heart

This form of criticism can come as a surprise or might blindside you. This type of criticisms usually comes from people whom you never thought important or never knew that they were keeping a tab on your life.

Though some of the times these criticisms do pay off but most of the times it is best not to pay any kind of attention on what they have to say. Even if you are right and doing something positive and great there will be people who will come and criticize your work.

In both the above mentioned examples keep in mind that your attitude should not under any circumstances be affected by the criticisms. Maintaining a constant positive attitude is a lot like when it rains outside. Just because it is raining outside does not necessarily imply that you would have to sit inside the room.

Rather you put on a raincoat or take an umbrella and go outside in spite of the rain. Similarly if criticisms starts showering upon you do not let that stop you from achieving any goal that you have set for yourself in your life.

You must keep a positive outlook. Maintaining this positive attitude would help you in keeping the criticisms out of your life.

Personality Style Differences Between Managers and Leaders

Managers and leader serve two distinct and separate functions within any organization. It is therefore important to keep in mind the required difference in the personality styles of these two roles.

The chief purpose of a manager is to ensure the proper operation of administrative processes in an organization and to thereby maximize its productive output.

A manager is required to maintain stability, discipline and control in the organization, and to solve problems with a view to the given operational structure, resources, goals and employee benefit. They are required to manage the problems that need to be resolved and optimize performance given the organizational restraints and to devise the best ways to do so.

Managers therefore tend to base their decisions more on the pressing and immediate needs of the day rather than long term goals and objectives.

Since they must necessarily focus on the current states of activities their decisions may often appear narrow; but it is also possible for them to look upon their work as an enabling process rather than one meant only for damage control. So, on their part, managers are good at working out short term strategies, negotiating compromises and mediating conflicts.

They can make valuable decisions by maneuvering people and ideas and by organizing and balancing contrary people and points of view.

Leaders, on the other hand, are generally conceived of as successful but lonely individuals. They have attained mastery over themselves and therefore can better control others while also creating for them a vision which infuses their work with value and direction.

Leaders are accordingly held to be imaginative, fervent and prone to taking risks; they are perceived to be proactive for promoting their ideas instead of simply reacting to the present situation.

They shed new light on long-standing problems and are engaged in developing their ideas and solutions. Similarly, leaders are seen as possessing the ability to relate to people in intuitive and empathetic ways, and to fill them with enthusiasm for their ideas.

Thus, a leader tends to be a new arrival to an organization, someone who has been imported for their vision, daring and innovation, but who may not necessarily have the experience or worldly prudence to implement the motion of change.

So whereas a leader is one who can instinctively command a following amongst employees and unite them for a common goal, a manager has to steadily work up the ladder and seek authority on the basis of their rooted and proven position in the company. A manager has to gain his standing through long and dependable service and effective organizational skills based on a clear understanding of how each level of the organization works.

Thus, managers and leaders adopt different approaches towards their goals. While the leader uses passion to generate emotion, the manager utilizes a more formal, rational method. But irrespective of these differences, successful managers and leaders both must seek to motivate and involve their employees.

If they can make the employee believe that he is appreciated and respected, and is a significant part of the organization, it is that much easier to inspire him and tap his potential.

Therefore it is vital for managers and leaders to involve employees in the process of making decisions and to inform them of any changes relevant to their position. Additionally, it is important for managers and leaders to remain approachable and available to employees and to show genuine interest in their needs.

All this generates a sense of security and belongingness in employees, making them want to work harder and contribute to the overall success of the organization.

Do You Have The Personality To Innovate?

The difference between an idea generator and a successful innovator lies in the latter's ability to undertake what is called "kaleidoscopic thinking". The first step towards creating a culture within the organization which is conducive to the fomenting of innovation is to identify employees who have the gift of kaleidoscopic thinking. We present nine traits which could help you identify the innovator amongst your people:

- **Curiosity is the basic component in innovation,** which makes the person question the status quo, seek new approaches and explanations and devise new solutions and pursue new possibilities. Not limiting themselves to the superficial aspect of things, they probe delve, imagining novel alternatives and paradigms.

- **Risk-taking and critical thinking.** But simply a curious and imaginative mentality does not an innovator make. It is necessary to be able to embrace risk and to be able to recognize the real possibilities of failure. Our experience with a number of our clients who are evaluating their leadership succession strength has revealed that many experienced managers, who have had to work their way up the ladder, become averse to risk with increasing stakes.

- **Resilience and Self-Control.** It is necessary that an innovation driven culture clearly acknowledge and build its function around the fact that many attempted innovations shall meet with failure. Many managers simply can't digest that, trying to negate any attendant risk and seeking a 95% guarantee that the proposed idea is actually going to hit off . this kills off rather than promotes innovation.

- **Interpersonal Skills**. Great innovative projects often frizzle out due to the failure to coordinate and communicate around the idea. This happens when the organizational charge is in the hands of the best techies rather than the best leaders. These technically oriented managers suppose that the innovative idea will automatically generate interest and motivation, and when they do try and communicate they do not try to attune their language to the sensibilities of their audiences, leaving them mystified.

- **Collaboration.** Innovate requires collaboration and teamwork. This is not a project specific endeavor but a spontaneous and continuous aspect of the work ethic. Best innovation proceeds from collective brain storming and a coordinated approach.

- **Dealing with Problems and Evolving Continually.** A final key element is the ability to handle complexity and adapt accordingly without wasting undue time. It is imperative to be able to meet up to the constant shifts and dynamism of the markets and the challenge of competition.

Innovation is incomplete if it doesn't match up to and outpace the competition, and if contingencies throw projects off track.

Assessing the actual preparedness for change and the conduciveness to innovation in your organization are necessary before declaring your company to be innovation driven. For if you do not have the proper people and the right environment to implement your business plan, your innovative vision will remain a dream.

Keep a Check on Your Attitude

It is quite a decent idea to keep a check on your attitude regularly. Certain attitudes must be checked; noticed and rectified otherwise they become our philosophy, which is dangerous.
Let's check some common attitude problems.

Anger

Anger is an inflated view of one's self and attitude.

Arrogance makes one deaf about other people's feelings, ideas or feedback. Arrogance is really a showcase of what we lack- genuine confidence. Genuine confidence gets you closer to other people arrogance takes you away.

Solution: God has given you three wonderful gifts- appreciation, confidence and humility. Practice them and you will go a long way.

EOE – Instant Expert On Everything

This is a person who has the answers to everything and is ready to speak about it at length (or a know-it-all).

IEOEs can be difficult to train or teach. Any relationship with this person, whether a friend, co worker or spouse is quite difficult. Ignorance is what you get if you are such a person.

Solution: Try developing a sense of curiosity for the world and its operations. Learn to say "I don't know" and then find answers.

Refusal of Taking Responsibility for Your Own Actions

If you do not take responsibility of your actions then it is a moral or emotional problem. If we do not take responsibility the power of changing things is also lost. Blaming others give them the power to change things and eradicate your problem-solving abilities.

Solution: when you are in trouble ask these three questions- What can I do? What can I read or know about? Whom shall I consult for expertise?

AAMS- the All about Me Syndrome

This is simply selfishness personified. There's a big difference between self care which is caring about one's self and being selfish which is me first and to heck with the rest.

Usually children have this behavior because it is natural during development. Growing up, means realizing that we are not the center of the universe.

Solution: Maintain a balance between taking care of you and noticing other people's lives and emotions.

Minimizing the Seriousness of Your Effect on Others

It is very easy to not notice what influence we are drawing up on others. If you are in any form of relationship what you do directly affects the other people around you. Not only your work but also your belief affects them.

Solution: Go back and see how others decisions have affected you. Then reflect on your actions and how they would have affected others.

How to Get Rid of Shyness

Shyness is not a handicap but it does hamper your personality's growth in the long run. It is for some indicative of lack of confidence in the self, for others it is the belief that they will never manage to break out so why try?

In other words both are indicative of your defeatist mentality.

So instead of merely envying your neighbor's grace and charm at conducting herself or himself at public gatherings, do away with that shyness now and try being the life of the party. Just consciously follow these few steps and see yourself emerging from behind that insecure shell.

And a final word of advice-don't give up trying that easily.

Venture out

For once lead a different life! If you are an average shy person, you must be spending your life hiding away form company, inside that apartment of yours. Well now is the time to give that unhealthy lifestyle up. Try going out and meeting new people. Remember that meeting new people helps you broaden your mind and learn more thereby enriching your life.

Get the Right Body Language

How you conduct yourself in public gatherings, your stance, your body language, your smile and talking style are all indicative of your shyness. Folding your arms in front and not smiling is a distinct signaling of your discomfort and your unwillingness to mingle and chat. So when in a party, make sure you walk around, smile, converse and in the end relax and have fun.

Give Those Personality Development Classes a Try

Thinking that you will never have it in you to be confident and bold? Well try some of those personality development classes to give you the boost you need. They will not only help you to mingle with others but also teach you how to conduct yourself and portray the right attitude in public gatherings. In the end you will be richer for your investment in these classes.

Keep on Trying

Nothing in life is minute made and similarly getting over your shyness will not happen magically in a day. So don't give up. There are many ways to overcoming your shyness and not all of them may work for you.

So keep giving all of them a try to see which one suits you the best. Remember no amount of guide and self help books can help you if you are not convinced that you can do it. So , go ahead with the never say die attitude and keep trying to get rid of your shyness no mater how disastrous your first attempt is.

So go ahead, make good use of these pointers and lead a more socially active life and you will se it will make you feel a lot more confident about yourself.

Printed in Great Britain
by Amazon